THE COAST OF NEW ENGLAND

A PICTORIAL TOUR FROM CONNECTICUT TO MAINE

Hadley Harbor

International Marine/
Ragged Mountain Press
A Division of The McGraw-Hill Companies

Published in the United States and its territories and Canada by International Marine,
a division of The McGraw-Hill Companies.

ISBN 0-07-048770-7

10 9 8 7 6 5 4 3 2 1

Questions regarding the ordering of this book should be addressed to:
The McGraw-Hill Companies
Customer Service Department
P.O. Box 547
Blacklick, OH 43004

Retail customers: 1-800-822-8158
Bookstores: 1-800-722-4726

Cover: Rockport, Massachusetts
Page 3 image: Rockport Harbor, Rockport, Massachusetts
Photographs were taken from May–September, 1995.

1. Coasts — New England — Pictorial works.
2. New England — Description and travel — Pictorial works.
I. Title.

THE COAST OF NEW ENGLAND

A PICTORIAL TOUR FROM CONNECTICUT TO MAINE

STAN PATEY

International Marine

Camden, Maine

THE NEW ENGLAND COAST

MAINE

Cobscook Bay

Chandler Bay

Dyers Bay

Frenchman Bay

Mount Desert Island

Penobscot Bay

Muscongus Bay

NEW HAMPSHIRE

Casco Bay

PORTLAND •

Saco Bay

• Portsmouth

Merrimack River

Ipswich Bay

Cape Ann

Connecticut River

MASSACHUSETTS

Massachusetts Bay

BOSTON•

Cape Cod Bay

RHODE ISLAND

Cape Cod

CONNECTICUT

PROVIDENCE •

Buzzards Bay

Nantucket Sound

Narragansett Bay

Rhode Island Sound

Martha's Vineyard

Nantucket

• **NEW HAVEN**

Long Island Sound

Block Island

Long Island

ATLANTIC OCEAN

CONTENTS

INTRODUCTION

FROM CONNECTICUT TO MAINE the course is "Down East" to the communities, harbors, rivers, inlets, beaches, and islands whose charm draws the sailor, tourist, and inhabitant alike to their beauty. Here, for the first time, you will find contemporary aerial and ground-based photography and charts that unlock the secrets and splendor of the New England coastline.

Our purpose in creating this pictorial guide is to provide a visual feast as well as a tool to those who would enhance their knowledge of coastal New England. It will serve as an inspiration and a preview to the traveler.

Those who inhabit this magnificent seaboard will find their homes, their communities, and their favorite locations. Your geographic connection to the surrounding waters and territories can be shared with family and friends.

Those who cruise the coastal waters on the hull of a boat, whether powered by motor or sail, will find the charts and photographs informative and comprehensive—as well as a vital aid to navigation. Readers can preview the entrances to harbors and inlets, and learn the locations of shallows, hazards, anchorages, marinas, and adjacent communities.

Hundreds of exciting destinations for those who travel the waters and shoreline of New England are featured. Preview your arrival at Mystic Seaport, Connecticut, with its collection of historic vessels and museums; then move on to the Elizabeth Islands separating Buzzards Bay and Vineyard Sound, or to the well-protected harbor of Oak Bluffs on the island of Martha's Vineyard. Here you will find the Methodist Meeting Grounds and the wonderful gingerbread houses that surround the tabernacle. Located at the edge of the harbor is one of

above: Mystic Harbor

left: Oak Bluffs

the oldest merry-go-rounds in the country with its hand-carved flying horses with traditional brass rings. A short walk along the edge of the harbor takes you to the sandy beaches and warm waters of Nantucket Sound.

Approximately twenty-five miles north of the Cape Cod Canal is New Inlet, which leads to the North and South Rivers. This passage should be negotiated only in calm weather as the current from the two rivers can result in both a very strong flow and steep seas. Spend an overnight in Humarock at the end of the South River and you will find anchorage, sand dunes, and beauty. The North River is bordered by marshes on both sides, and offers one small boatyard and little in the way of facilities. Swimming at the junction of the North and South Rivers is dangerous because of the strong currents. However, if you turn from New Inlet into the South River, you will find good swimming at Humarock's public beach. The town of Humarock offers marinas, restaurants, groceries, and a small interesting vacationer's village.

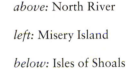

above: North River

left: Misery Island

below: Isles of Shoals

Northeast of New Inlet, past Boston Harbor and its multitude of interesting and historic islands, are the anchorage and lovely trails of Misery Island. Located in Salem Sound between Marblehead Harbor and Manchester Harbor, Massachusetts, the island offers swimming and a memorable experience.

Continue your trip past Cape Ann, Massachusetts to the Isles of Shoals, located twelve miles off the coast of Portsmouth, New Hampshire, and divided by the border between New Hampshire and Maine. Here you will find seven islands, including Appledore, Smuttynose, and Star, that offer hiking, swimming, historic buildings, gruesome stories, bird rookeries, and rugged beauty as well as the remote, picturesque anchorage of Gosport Harbor.

In the southeastern portion of Maine's Casco Bay can be found Jewell Island, a state park with a long slender harbor and many hiking trails. Walk to the southern end of the island and climb the two observation towers which overlook the vast expanse of Casco Bay and its 365 Calendar Islands. Investigate the linked tunnels which during World War II supported 16-inch guns that protected the entrance to Portland Harbor. Swim in the Punch Bowl that fills with Maine's cold salt water at high tide and warms up for your swimming pleasure as the tide recedes.

below: Jewell Island

For those who reach Mount Desert Island in eastern Maine, a crowning experience can be the seven mile sail up Somes Sound. A place to pause is Valley Cove on the west side. Here you can anchor or pick up one of the park service's free moorings. Row ashore to one of the hiking trails that will take you to the summit of Saint Sauveur Mountain for an unforgettable view, or take the trail that winds up to the top of Acadia Mountain. The wild flower gardens of Fernald Point and the Robert Abbe Museum also provide interesting visits.

For those who travel by boat, on the four wheels of an automobile, or in any recreational vehicle, this book is a preview of the historic and enchanting communities of the coast of New England. See the beaches, rivers, and inlets that attracted the early settlers. Gain the insight to select that most special locale to add to your family memoirs.

above: Somes Sound

CHAPTER ONE

THE COAST OF CONNECTICUT

LONG ISLAND SOUND FROM GREENWICH HARBOR TO THE MYSTIC RIVER

Shown here are the Thimble Islands

THE CONNECTICUT COAST

CONNECTICUT

Mianus River

Norwalk River

Saugatuck River

Mill River

Pequonnock River

Housatonic River

Branford River

FAIR HAVEN

NEW HAVEN

WEST HAVEN

New Haven Harbor

EAST HAVEN

BRANFORD

23-24

25

Thimble Isl.

19-20

MILFORD

STRATFORD

22

Milford Harbor

BRIDGEPORT

21

Bridgeport Harbor

18

SOUTHPORT

Black Rock Harbor

16-17

18

19-20

NORWALK

Norwalk Harbor

ROWAYTON

16

STAMFORD

14

COS COB

15

Stamford Harbor

GREENWICH

12-14

Greenwich Harbor
Cos Cob Harbor
Greenwich Cove

Long Island Sound

Long Island

NEW YORK

Connecticut River

Hamburg Cove

32

ESSEX •

Hammonasset River

West River

East River

Niantic River

Thames River

Mystic River

Pawcatuck River

39-42

29-30

WESTBROOK

LYME

36

NIANTIC

NEW
LONDON

• GROTON

• MYSTIC

STONINGTON

CLINTON

SAYBROOK

NOANK

Little
Narragansett
Bay

Westbrook
Harbor

Niantic
Bay

37-38

Fishers Island
Sound

43-44

FORD •
hem
d Guilford
Harbor

Duck Island
Roads

28

29-31

Clinton
Harbor

33-35

Fishers Island

Block Island
Sound

26-27

Plum Island

ATLANTIC OCEAN

right inset: The Indian Harbor Yacht Club (featured in this photo) was built in 1919. Greenwich has been and still is known as a top-notch yachting center. Located on the shores of Long Island Sound, Greenwich was settled in the second half of the seventeenth century.

above: Old Greenwich and Stamford shelter behind the spit that reaches out to create Greenwich Cove. Although it lacks any shoreside facilities, Greenwich Cove is a safe, pleasant anchorage when weather deteriorates. Its popularity, however, makes space somewhat scarce.

left: The man-made breakwater continues the extension of land that is Byram Point and creates further protection for Port Chester Harbor on the western side of Captain Harbor. Beware of Manursing Island Reef near the entrance of the harbor, though.

left: The outer anchorage of Greenwich Harbor, known as Captain Harbor (foreground), is easy to enter, use, and leave in normal summer weather. In poor weather, though, the inner harbor of Bush Cove (upper left) is best for deep-draft boats, while Smith Cove and Indian Harbor (upper center and upper right) can accommodate a few extra shoal-draft vessels.

above: Greenwich Cove (left foreground), Cos Cob Harbor (right), Greenwich Harbor (right background), and Port Chester Harbor (middle background), all lie within the greater waters of Captain Harbor.

above: The Mianus River pours into Cos Cob Harbor. The lifting bridge crossing the Mianus River can cause delays and the fixed highway bridge restricts mast height to 45 feet. But the harbor is an otherwise easy way to enjoy the numerous marinas and yacht clubs of boating-focused Cos Cob.

right: This restored building in Greenwich was known as Knapp's Tavern during the American Revolution. When the British attacked the colonial town in 1779, General Israel Putnam used the structure as his head-quarters. The historic landmark, now called Putnam Cottage, was built in 1699. It is noted for its unusual scalloped shingles.

above: The breakwaters (foreground) of the outer anchorage to Stamford Harbor make the haven useful to heavy pleasure and commercial traffic. Southerly and southwesterly winds force most small craft to retreat to the inner harbors.

left: The inner harbors at Stamford are known as the West Branch (at right) and East Branch (at left). Both bring you into the heart of the city, with facilities galore. The hurricane gate of the East Branch provides maximum protection from extreme weather conditions.

15

right: The watery entrance to Rowayton and Darien, Five Mile River is easy to enter for all but the deepest draft vessels. For those deep draft vessels, enter on the rising seven-foot tides.

left: The Norwalk Islands (at right) form southerly protection for greater Norwalk Harbor and are best explored in a shoal draft vessel. Many islanders jealously guard their privacy, so landing is limited. Scott Cove (foreground), Five Mile River (near left), and the Norwalk River (center), lie west of Fairfield in the distance.

right: With 11 possible berthing areas, Norwalk Harbor is a justifiably popular stopover for transient sailors. If in doubt about overnight anchoring or tie-ups, the harbormaster always monitors VHF radio calls and is very accommodating. The entrance channel appears in the foreground.

below: The quaint Sheffield Island Lighthouse in Norwalk looks out toward 16 small islands off the Connecticut coast. The islands range in size from one to 70 acres and stretch over six miles.

left: Wilson Cove (foreground) is one of the most popular anchorages in Norwalk (background). Easy to enter and well dredged, it is the home of the Norwalk Yacht Club.

right: Sheffield Island (distance). Chimon Island (center), and Cockenoe Island (foreground), are three of the sixteen Norwalk Islands. Sheffield Island on the south side of Norwalk Harbor is a popular anchorage in settled weather. Landing is tricky with part of the island private, part nature preserve, and part available for a casual walk.

left: Compo Yacht Basin is in the bight behind sandy Cedar Point. The beach and marina are very popular and busy spots all summer.

below: Seymour Point (at right) is opposite Cedar Point at the mouth of the Saugatuck River, and also contains tie-up facilities. Additional facilities are scarce farther upriver.

right: The Mill River has made Southport yet another "perfectly protected" harbor on Connecticut's south shore. Space is scarce, though, and shoal spots can catch the unwary.

left inset: Captain's Cove Seaport is home to the tall ship H.M.S. *Rose,* the largest operational sailing ship in the world. Settled in 1639, Bridgeport quickly became a major port of entry for the state and thrived during the Industrial Revolution. Bridgeport is the hometown of P.T. Barnum, the great showman, and the birthplace of General Tom Thumb, the 28-inch tall Barnum performer.

above: Bridgeport's main harbor is primarily concerned with commercial traffic, though plenty of pleasure craft also call it home. The breakwaters of Bridgeport Harbor create a grand entranceway to Yellow Mill Channel, Johnsons Creek, and the cities of Bridgeport and Newfield. The secondary shelter of Black Rock Harbor (see next page) is two miles westward of the city's twin breakwaters, and is the more popular pleasure boat haven for boats visiting Bridgeport.

above: Beyond the light at Penfield Reef (lower left) is the haven of Black Rock Harbor (upper right). Easy to find and enter in all weather, day or night, it boasts numerous facilities, mainly near the tributary of Burr Creek.

right: The distinctive red-and-white-striped power plant smokestack on Tongue Point at Bridgeport has long been a significant landmark for mariners all over Long Island Sound. Other stacks on Steel Point and power line towers make the harbor unmistakable from sea. Long Island appears in the distance in this photo.

left: The Housatonic River and Stratford appear to be part of Bridgeport in this photo, but the Housatonic is far less urban in appearance and pace, as is the town of Stratford.

below: Entering the Housatonic River via the breakwater is best done on a flood tide, which can run up to four knots. The marshes of the lower river make it seem almost rural.

above: Simple to enter, Milford Harbor is usually busy with small racing fleets of Lasers, Lightnings, 210s, and so forth. It's best to give them a wide berth.

left: Though there is little room to anchor, Milford Harbor often has a spare guest mooring available on weekdays. If anchoring, watch the depths carefully; there is shoaling in this twisted entrance.

right: This nineteenth-century lighthouse stands on the shores of Long Island Sound, where Reverend John Davenport and a band of Puritans founded New Haven in 1638. The lighthouse is now surrounded by an 80-acre historic park. Five miles south of town, New Haven Harbor remains a bustling port for commercial ships and private boats. New Haven is the home of Yale University.

above: Though the view from this southern vantage shows that the harbor of New Haven is vast, the breakwaters knock down the worst seas. West River (left center) and Morris Cove (right) offer more protection, some amenities and access to the busy cities of New Haven (left) and Fair Haven (right).

above: The industrial waterfront at Fair Haven on the Quinnipiac River offers pleasure boats the spectacle of a working waterfront, but dallying is not recommended.

left: A statue of Nathan Hale in New Haven commemorates that patriot's brave proclamation of regret at having "but one life to give for my country." In 1779, 19 patriots at Black Rock Fort on the east side of the harbor bravely resisted the three thousand British and German Hessian troops who eventually captured this important port town.

left: A few miles east of the city, Branford Harbor is where the yachting crowd of the greater New Haven area generally keeps their boats. The Thimble Islands appear in the background to the east.

below: Although the Branford Harbor channel looks tortuous, it is easy to follow. Engineless sailboats have been known to enter and leave the Branford River with ease.

left: The prominent Brewer's marina at the horseshoe bend in the Branford River is a haven primarily for sailboats, while numerous other marinas welcome power boats or a mix of the two. New Haven is in the distance.

THIMBLE ISLANDS AND SACHEM HEAD

below inset: A northerly look from 1000 feet shows Sachem Head (left), Sachem Head Harbor (left background), and Joshua Cove (right foreground). Sachem Head is small and difficult to enter at night. But if the wind is northwest or easterly, it makes a very pleasant little rural harbor.

below: The Thimble Islands between Branford and Sachem Head make an interesting diversion, primarily because they give a hint of what cruising farther north and east is like. Residents, however, guard their privacy jealously.

above: Some of the Thimble islets are barely large enough for a single house. Others accommodate numerous homes. Architectural styles range from modern to English manor and Victorian.

left: The unmarked islets around the Thimble Islands, such as this one, make navigation treacherous. In the late 1600s, Captain Kidd reputedly hid out on one of the islands before he was captured.

below: Anchoring is not recommended at Sachem Head Harbor because of the rocky nature of the bottom. But moorings are generally available if you ask someone ashore. Indian Cove (left) and Guilford Harbor (left background) appear in the distance.

below inset: The Thimble Islands were named for the thimble-berries that once thrived on them. An oyster industry and granite quarries formerly prospered in this small, rocky archipelago.

below: This view of the entrance to Guilford Harbor, shows Mulberry Point (center), Indian Cove (left), and the West River (right). Guilford Harbor makes an attractive, restful stopover for a shoal draft boat. Deep draft boats must follow the channel carefully on a rising tide.

right inset: Guilford's founder, the Reverend Henry Whitfield, lived in this house, said to be New England's oldest stone dwelling. Now a museum, the house is fully restored and furnished with seventeenth century antiques. The village green of this quiet town—bordered by churches, stately homes, and public buildings—dates back to Guilford's beginning in 1639, and was once the center of community activity.

left inset: Clinton Harbor is another haven that tends to shoal in, but is worth visiting anyway. The Hammonasset River provides a pleasant waterfront for a relatively quiet town.

below: Westbrook Harbor, the Patchogue River (right), and the Menunketesuck River (left), make an excellent alternative to the dubious anchorage at nearby Duck Island Roads. Arrive early to assure a berth.

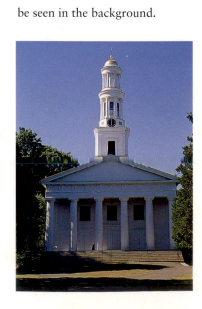

above: Duck Island, the break-water, and Duck Island Roads are worth a visit if the weather is settled. Westbrook Harbor can be seen in the background.

above inset: The outer break-water near Clinton Harbor (at left) should be used as protection only if there is absolutely no other alternative. Head for the Hammonasset River and the inner harbor if possible.

right: Sailors, for years, have used the gold dome of the First Congregational Church in Madison, west of Clinton Harbor, as a landmark.

right: At Westbrook Harbor, the Menunketesuck River (at right) is a good alternative to the Patchogue River, which tends to fill up with transient traffic first. Duck Island Roads is in the distance.

below: Boaters must pass Cedar Island (center) in Clinton Harbor to reach the Hammonasset River.

HAMBURG COVE

Travel six miles north into the Connecticut River, pass Saybrook (Essex will be to your west), and turn east at Brockway Island. After passing through the narrow channel leading to the northeast, you will emerge into the small basin and classic New England village of Hamburg. The Lower Cove is one of the most desirable anchorages anywhere. Clearly a well protected hurricane hole, this tranquil anchorage is often selected by those who know the locality for rafting get-togethers. Surrounded by hills and trees and a quaint New England village, you have found an ideal spot to pause on your trip. The town is small, the swimming is great, and the traditional New England country store, well known for delicious ice cream, is conveniently situated at the head of the cove.

above: Essex (left foreground) is a popular harbor for transient sailors visiting the Connecticut River (right). Anchoring must be done with caution, since the currents are formidable.

right: The Florence Griswold Museum housed America's first art colony, which included the artists Childe Hassam, Willard Metcalf, and other American Barbizon Impressionists. The handsome Georgian-style mansion, built in 1817 in the early harbor town of Old Lyme, today houses Impressionist paintings.

right: The Saybrook Outer Bar Channel is shared by pleasure and commercial traffic. In thick weather, proceed carefully and watch for tugs with barges.

below: The Connecticut River is navigable inland as far as the city of Hartford. The trip is mostly bucolic with good facilities all the way.

right inset: Located at the foot of Main Street in an old warehouse, the Connecticut River Museum in Essex explores the river's history. Displays illustrate shipbuilding and maritime life, and include shipbuilding tools and half-models and full-rigged models of ships that sailed along New England's longest river. Of particular interest is a life-size replica of the first submarine—David Bushnell's *American Turtle*—invented to sink British ships in the Revolution. This white building appears on the museum grounds.

right: Visitors to the Connecticut River Museum can stroll the nearby docks and watch the procession of boats that now sail the river. The town of Essex, formerly a notable shipbuilding center, is now a yachting port.

above: The town of Essex makes a major effort to accommodate pleasure traffic in the Connecticut River. Chandleries, brokerages, restaurants, and marinas make it an entertaining stop.

above: Boats sometimes anchor near Crescent Beach, on the west shore of Niantic Bay. This is sensible only in calm weather and well away from swimming areas.

right inset: Entering Niantic's inner harbor is made difficult by bridges, currents, shoaling, and heavy pleasure traffic. The bar stretches across the Niantic River. Once inside, facilities are good. The town of Niantic is off the left edge of this view upriver.

left: The Thomas Lee House, built in 1660, is one of Connecticut's oldest wooden-frame houses still on the original site. Nearby stands the Little Boston School, which was the first district school between New York and Boston. Both buildings contain period furnishings.

above: New London (at right) and Groton (at left) share the easily entered Thames River.

right: The U.S. Coast Guard Academy is on the New London side of the Thames River. If you're lucky, you might see their square-rigged *Eagle* departing or returning.

left inset: The USS *Nautilus*, the world's first nuclear-powered submarine, is part of the USS *Nautilus* Memorial/Submarine Force Library and Museum in Groton, Connecticut. The 519-foot-long submarine was built in 1954 at Groton's General Dynamics Electric Boat Division shipyard and was christened by Mamie Eisenhower. The museum examines the history of underwater navigation and displays models of every class of submarine built.

above: Avery Point and Shenecosset are featured in this scene along with the end of the runway of the Groton/New London Airport.

MYSTIC

After entering Mystic Harbor, beyond charming Noank to the west and Mason Island to the east, pass through the railroad bridge and you will arrive at Mystic Seaport. Here you find the Mystic Seaport's celebrated collection of historic vessels including the square-rigged *Charles W. Morgan*, a classic and well-known whaling vessel, the time-honored *Joseph Conrad*, a nineteenth century square-rigged sailing vessel, the Grand Banks fishing schooner *L.A. Dunton*, 12 meter sloops, and many other tall ships and powerboats. The exhibits and captivating nautical displays are well worth many hours of viewing. The museum houses one of the largest collections of wooden vessels, art collections, an important marine library, a planetarium, and programs including boatbuilding, and nautical history. The Mystic Marine Life Aquarium, north of the Seaport, displays over 6,000 specimens of marine life in over forty exhibits.

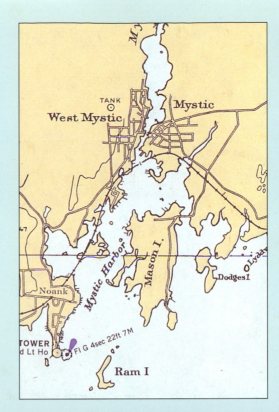

right inset: The lower Mystic River marks the beginning of a transient mariner's ascent to "sailor's heaven" at Mystic Seaport, famous for its presentation of America's maritime heritage.

below: Although a long, twisting way inland from Long Island Sound, the trip upriver to Mystic is nearly always worth the effort.

below inset: Noank (left) and Mason Island (right) can be found near the mouth of the Mystic River. It is surprisingly easy to get an overnight berth in a port as popular as Mystic. The farther downriver you are, the easier it is to find space.

above: The tide-scoured waters of Fisher's Island Sound lead to the various anchorages of Mystic. Be careful in foggy weather.

below: This photograph shows the town of Mystic from the west.

above inset: Mystic was one of the busiest ports on the Eastern seaboard in the eighteenth and nineteenth centuries. Some of the fastest clipper ships on the Atlantic were built there. The flourishing boat and shipbuilding industry declined in the 1880s. Today, Mystic is known for its Seaport Museum, the largest maritime museum in the country. Shown here is the *L.A. Dunton*.

above: The Pawcatuck River, east of Mystic, marking the eastern limit of Connecticut waters, is a stop worth making. Most facilities are on the Rhode Island side of the river.

left inset: Restoration Shipyard docks the schooner *L. A. Dunton* and the steamship *Sabino.*

below: Be patient with the bridge at Mystic. It opens on a set schedule, and the bridgetender can be contacted on VHF channel 13.

left: Stonington's lighthouse was the first constructed by the federal government. Built in 1823, the stone structure now houses the Old Lighthouse Museum. The museum displays town relics, including the daily log of an old sailing ship and a ballot box containing white marbles for casting "yes" votes and black ones for "no" votes. Stonington, a thriving fishing village, was settled in 1735.

right inset: The breakwaters at Stonington are well lighted and offer excellent protection.

below: Stonington has become a major pleasure boat harbor because of its safety, ease of entering, and proximity to well-known ports east and south.

above: The best anchoring spots in Stonington Harbor depend on the wind's direction. Thanks to breakwaters and the harbor's natural shape and depth, you can always find space well under the lee of solid protection.

right: Stonington Point divides the harbor (center) from Little Narragansett Bay (lower right) and the entrance to the Pawcatuck River. Mystic Harbor is in the distance.

CHAPTER TWO

RHODE ISLAND WATERS

WATCH HILL TO THE SAKONNET RIVER, INCLUDING
BLOCK ISLAND AND NARRAGANSETT BAY

Shown here is Tiverton Narrows

RHODE ISLAND WATERS

MASSACHUSETTS

RHODE ISLAND

• PROVIDENCE

• FALL RIVER

58

55

Horse Neck

Warwick Cove

Narragansett Bay

Mount Hope Bay

Apponaug Cove

Warwick Neck

54-55

Greenwich Bay

Greenwich Cove

Patience Island

Popasquash Neck

BRISTOL

Bristol Neck

Bristol Harbor

58

52

Allen Harbor

Hog Island

56-57

• TIVERTON

WICKFORD •

Hope Island

PORTSMOUTH

52-53

Prudence Island

• MELVILLE

57

West Passage

East Passage

Aquidneck Island

Conanicut Island

63-64

Sakonnet River

Dutch Island

JAMESTOWN

59-62

Newport Harbor

• NEWPORT

Beaver Neck

Newport Neck

Sakonnet Point

65-66

Point Judith Pond

Rhode Island Sound

SNUG HARBOR •

JERUSALEM •

• GALILEE

51

Point Judith Harbor of Refuge

• POINT JUDITH

50

ATLANTIC OCEAN

48-49

WATCH HILL

Block Island Sound

47

Great Salt Pond

Old Harbor

Block Island

right: At 600 feet, this picture shows the more popular haven of Great Salt Pond in the foreground and the distinctive jetties of Old Harbor in the distance on the opposite side of Block Island.

below: Great Salt Pond on the west side of Block Island is good shelter in all but strong northerly winds. Currents in the narrow entrance are manageable.

right: Used mainly by sport and commercial fishermen, plus the regular ferry to Block Island, Old Harbor offers good protection in normal summer weather. Unfortunately, anchoring is prohibited.

above: Just east of Connecticut and south of the Pawcatuck River lies Watch Hill. From this vantage point over the river we look west over Little Narragansett Bay (foreground) and Stonington Harbor (left middle) all the way to Mystic Harbor, Connecticut.

above inset: For more than 150 years, the Watch Island Lighthouse has shone its light over Block Island Sound. The lighthouse stands on the shore of Watch Hill Point in Westerly, a busy nineteenth century railroad town. Near the lighthouse is the Watch Hill Carousel, with its enchanting handcarved horses that hang from chains and fly out as the carousel turns. Built in 1867, the carousel is said to be one of the country's oldest.

above: The harbor at Watch Hill is a sandy pleasure. The protective isthmus on the harbor's south side features Napatree Beach, which offers excellent, warm saltwater swimming, and separates Watch Hill Harbor from Block Island Sound.

above: The Harbor of Refuge at Pt. Judith is well placed for the benefit of mariners seeking shelter from heavy weather. The inner harbor (right) offers the best protection.

right: The original wooden lighthouse at Point Judith, Rhode Island, was destroyed by a hurricane in 1815, five years after it was built. A new tower of rough stone, 35 feet in height, was constructed in its place. That tower had a revolving light made of 10 lamps and reflectors that operated with a simple power mechanism. In 1871, sea captains requested that the fog signal be changed from a horn to a whistle. The whistle was more easily heard over the sound of the surf, and could easily be distinguished from the sound of the Beavertail Lighthouse's siren.

left: This is another view of the Point Judith Lighthouse, which stands on a natural site extending out at the junction of Narragansett Bay and Long Island Sound. In 1907, 22,680 vessels were counted passing the lighthouse during the daytime, and twice that many were estimated to have passed at night.

above: The inner harbor at Pt. Judith features extensive commercial piers of Jerusalem (top left), Snug Harbor (top right), and Galilee (bottom). The best anchorage is beyond the piers in Pt. Judith Pond.

above: Wickford's harbor is popular because of its excellent protection, and a town whose quiet charm and convenience just won't quit. After entering between the breakwaters, Wickford Cove is to your left, Mill Creek is ahead, and Fishing Cove is to the right.

right: Between Spink Neck (left) and Calf Pasture Point (right) is the entrance to Allen Harbor, which offers good protection but little room for anchoring.

right inset: Wickford, in the southwestern corner of Rhode Island on Narragansett Bay, looks out on its beautiful harbor filled with fishing boats and pleasure craft. The town, known for its abundant craft and antique shops, is the setting of John Updike's novel *The Witches of Eastwick*.

above: When heavy easterlies threaten, Wickford Cove (middle foreground) offers the best protection. Cornelius Island and Point Wharf are on the left side of the photograph

above: Apponaug Cove (right) is in the northwest corner of Greenwich Bay. Restaurants, marinas, and a nearby major airport are its most important facilities.

right inset: The moorings and slips at Greenwich Cove's inner harbor are comfortable in all but strong southerly winds.

left inset: Potter Cove, on Prudence Island, offers excellent protection, a couple of state-maintained moorings, and no facilities. Its charm is in its rustic nature. Beyond Prudence Island to the northwest lie Patience Island and Greenwich Bay.

below: Warwick Cove is closely guarded by Horse Neck (left) and Warwick Neck.

below: Although open to southerly winds, Bristol Harbor remains popular because of its historically long love affair with pleasure boats.

right: The Herreshoff Marine Museum in Bristol, Rhode Island, displays an excellent collection of boats, engines and fittings, and a wonderful assortment of photographs of ships and their captains. Museum displays depict the accomplishments of the Herreshoff Manufacturing Company during the nineteenth and twentieth centuries. The Herreshoff Boatyard built some of the fastest and most sophisticated yachts in America. Yachts produced by the Herreshoff family, still involved in sailing, have won numerous prestigious races, including the America's Cup.

left: The Blithewold Gardens and Arboretum in Bristol, Rhode Island, abound with exotic shrubs and trees that were just being introduced to the United States from Japan and China when the gardens were designed in the late 1800s. Yellow-groove bamboo, Japanese cedar, and a weeping pagoda tree are a sampling of the garden's grounds, which also includes rose, rock, and water gardens. The 33-acre property is the former summer estate of Pennsylvania coal baron Augustus Van Wickle. The house, built in 1895, was patterned after an English country manor. The name "Blithewold" means "cheerful place" in Old English.

below: Making a harbor where natural forces neglected to do so, Little Harbor Marine on the northwest shore of Aquidneck Island is always popular.

right: This Civil War monument commemorates the people of Bristol, Rhode Island's involvement in the Civil War. One of the men is a sailor, and the other a soldier. The statue is framed from behind by Saint Michaels Chapel in the center of town.

above: Tiverton Narrows, Rhode Island (foreground), creates a harbor used extensively by residents of Rhode Island and the greater Fall River, Massachusetts, area (background). Mt Hope Bay is at center left with the Tauton River top center.

right inset: The city of Fall River, Massachusetts, with Battleship Cove offers history buffs plenty to see, with a World War II battleship, destroyer, submarine, and PT boat, plus a general maritime history museum.

above: Dutch Island Harbor is a large, handy haven for sailors interested in the shops of Jamestown. Newport is in the distance.

left inset: With Jamestown to port and Newport to starboard, the lighthouse at Castle Hill (center bottom) is a landmark thousands of sailors use every year.

right inset: This colorful Chinese Tea House on the Marble House grounds in Newport was designed by Richard Morris Hunt for William Vanderbilt in 1892. The tea house stands close to the Cliff Walk that winds around the property. The Marble House, with its two-story portico constructed with six great Corinthian columns, was patterned after the Grand and Petit Trianons at Versailles.

right: Newport retains its reputation for a racing sailor's premier harbor, as well as an excellent anchorage for transient sailors. All imaginable facilities are available. A J-boat passes Fort Adams.

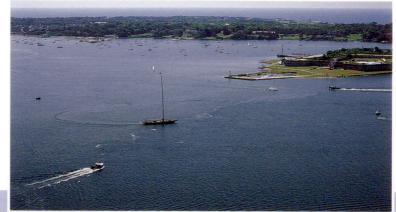

above: Newport Neck extends to the west at the southern end of Aquidnick Island, creating protection for Newport Harbor. The smaller Goat Island is shown in the distance.

left: This Victorian mansion, built in 1852, was enlarged by noted architect Richard Morris Hunt 20 years later. It was his first commission in the High Victorian grand manner. Unlike many of the Newport mansions, this was a year-round rather than a summer residence. Images of birds, plants, and sky adorn painted ceilings inside the mansion, and a mural of the "Tree of Life" accompanies the staircase. Richard Morris Hunt, in addition to designing several Rhode Island mansions, also designed the New York Public Library and the pedestal of the Statue of Liberty.

right: The Breakers in Newport, modeled after a northern Italian Renaissance villa, was designed by Richard Morris Hunt in 1895 for Cornelius Vanderbilt, who used it for 10 weeks each summer. The elaborate mansion was built by 2,500 workers, who labored for two years. Marble columns, towers, and double loggias decorate the façade. The breathtaking mansion contains an immense hall of Caen marble and a formal dining room resplendent with alabaster pillars, murals, and chandeliers.

above: Brenton Cove (foreground) lies near the entrance to busy Newport Harbor.

above: Newport's inner harbor and city (foreground) behind Goat Island (middle right) is busy day and night, all summer long. Call ahead and arrive early if you need a berth here.

left inset: This statue of General Rochambeau stands at the spot where the French general arrived in Newport with 5,000 French troops during the Revolutionary War. Rochambeau and the French Army helped the American colonists drive the English out of Newport.

above: The White Horse Tavern, in Newport, Rhode Island, is the oldest tavern in America. A special state law was passed to ensure that the White Horse could continue to renew its liquor license, which neighboring churches had tried to stop. The law gives special privilege to taverns built before 1700 with a church on either side. The tavern survived threats of demolition in the 1950s, and continues to serve customers today.

right: The ease with which you leave and enter Dutch Island Harbor on Conanicut Island makes it a favorite stop for large fleets of cruising sailboats. Five state-maintained moorings are available here.

below: Jamestown Harbor is a good haven when westerly winds blow and nearby Newport appears a bit too crowded.

right: Built in 1749, the Beavertail Lighthouse in Jamestown, Rhode Island, reputedly is the third lighthouse erected in the United States. The lighthouse, still in use today, houses a small museum. The original 69-foot wooden tower burned to the ground only three years after it was built. It was replaced by a 64-foot wood and stone tower, which was later badly damaged in the Revolutionary War and was again rebuilt. A hurricane in 1815 destroyed the tower yet again, and Congress appropriated funds in the mid-1800s to build the granite tower that stands today.

above: The portion of Jamestown Harbor defined by Bull Point (lower left) and the Dumplings (islands to the right) must be navigated with care to avoid shoals and rocks.

above: Sakonnet Point and
Sakonnet Harbor behind it make
a convenient—if small—harbor
for boats bound east and west
along the Rhode Island coast.

above: Despite the breakwater, a swell can work into parts of Sakonnet Harbor. Still, the stop is worthwhile and the ambience is relaxed. Round Pond and the Atlantic Ocean can be seen in the background.

right: Looking north up the Sakonnet River, this photograph shows Tiverton Narrows in the distance.

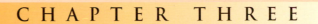

CHAPTER THREE

MASSACHUSETTS WATERS SOUTH OF THE CAPE

WESTPORT THROUGH THE SOUTHERN CAPE,
INCLUDING BUZZARDS BAY,
MARTHA'S VINEYARD, AND NANTUCKET

Cuttyhunk

MASSACHUSETTS WATERS
SOUTH OF THE CAPE

MASSACHUSETTS

Wareham River

76 • WAREHAM ONSET

Cape Cod Canal

Onset Bay

77

Achushnet River

Sippican Neck

MARION •

74 **75**

77 **78** • MONUMENT BE

Sippican Harbor

79-80 • POCASSET

Red Brook Harbor • CATAUMET

NEW BEDFORD

73

• MATTAPOISETT

• FAIRHAVEN

Mattapoisett Neck

Mattapoisett Harbor

• WESTPORT

PADANARUM (SOUTH DARTMOUTH)

72

Apponagansett Bay

87

FALMOUTH

Westport River

Westport Point

70-71

Westport Harbor

Horseneck Point

Buzzards Bay

81 Quissett Harbor

WOODS HOLE

Great Pond

84 Hadley Harbor

Falmouth Harbor

86

Nonamesset Island

82-83

Naushon Island

Elizabeth Islands

95

96-97

85

Pasque Island

VINEYARD HAVEN

OAK BLUFFS

Cuttyhunk Harbor

Nashawena Island

Vineyard Sound

Cuttyhunk Island

Martha's Vineyard

EDGART

94-95

94

• MENEMSHA

Gay Head

Menemsha Pond

ATLANTIC

Cape Cod Bay

Cape Cod

Chatham
Harbor

North   Bay

89

Cotuit
Bay

West
Bay

90

WEST YARMOUTH

● HYANNIS

● BASS RIVER

● HARWICH

92-93

Stage
Harbor

● CHATHAM

92-93

● OSTERVILLE

Hyannis
Harbor

Lewis
Bay

**Parker
River**

91

Wychmere
Harbor

92

Chatham
Roads

89

Popponesset
Bay

91

88

97

Edgartown
Harbor

Nantucket Sound

98

Nantucket
Harbor

Nantucket

above: Horseneck Beach on Horseneck Point breaks the mouth of the Westport River and creates the entrance to Westport Harbor. The Elizabeth Islands are visible in the distance.

right inset: The Atlantic can be seen behind Horseneck Beach and the town of Westport Point. Curves in the channel at Westport can be tricky. Sometimes the current runs with the channel, sometimes across it.

below: The tidal currents at the mouth of Westport Harbor are strong, and low-power auxiliaries should avoid trying to buck them. If you must wait to get in, it's worth it.

above: Racing fleets, sailing equipment, and old time sailors are found in abundance at Padanaram, also known as South Dartmouth, on Apponagansett Bay. The boatyards (at lower left) are also rated top-notch.

right inset: The approach to Apponagansett Bay and Padanaram is easy, but it does allow wind and waves to keep the harbor fairly stirred up.

left: This statue on the waterfront in New Bedford commemorates the fact that New Bedford was once the whaling capital of the world. The two-masted schooner *Ernestina* sits behind the statue in the still busy waterfront.

below: The hurricane barrier at New Bedford (left) and Fairhaven (right) provide a safe harbor in all weathers. Home of Joshua Slocum, the area touts its pleasure boat heritage as well as its commercial maritime roots.

above: In the southwest corner of Nasketucket Bay, southwest of Mattapoisett, is excellent protection for shoal draft vessels only. The marina pictured between Sconticut Neck (right) and West Island (left) is best for tying up to a dock.

below: Although boatyards in Mattapoisett are few, they have most goods and services a transient sailor might need.

above: Mattapoisett, nestled between Mattapoisett Neck and Strawberry Point, is another yachting harbor that is susceptible to problems when the wind turns southerly. Hurricane Bob ravaged the area in 1991. But in normal summer weather, it's fine.

above inset: Ned's Point Lighthouse and Park guard the mouth of Mattapoisett Harbor. The natural beauty of this park is only enhanced by its panoramic view of Buzzards Bay.

left: The first boats are just beginning the first leg of the 1995 Marion to Bermuda Race in Sippican Harbor. The boats must first pass Ram Island and Planting Cove.

above: Ram Island is in the foreground of this view of Sippican Harbor and the town of Marion.

left: Marion was named after the Revolutionary War hero General Frances Marion, the "Swamp Fox." This carefully tended town, however, is anything but swampy. Buzzards Bay can be seen in the background.

75

right inset: Currents in the Wareham River can run up to four knots in the narrow spots. But the facilities at Wareham itself are worth the effort.

This view of the Wareham River, from Wareham Neck to Swifts Beach, includes the Broad Marsh River.

above: The twisting channel to Onset Harbor is easy to follow. The harbor itself is well protected, full of diversions and a convenient place to wait for a favorable tide in the Cape Cod Canal. Hog Neck, Burgess Point, and Onset Island are near the front of Onset Bay in the photo, while Jacobs Neck and Wickets Island lie in the background.

right: Crooked River (lower right) and Broad Marsh River (middle left) twist away from Inner Wareham Harbor.

left: The best holding ground in Onset Bay is between Wickets Island (center) and Onset Island (center foreground). The depths are around eight feet. Be sure to hang out an anchor light at night. The town of Onset spreads out around the bay with Point Independence to the right of Wickets Island.

below: The Massachusetts Maritime Academy is on Taylor Point (center) at the west, or Buzzards Bay, end of the Cape Cod Canal. Most traffic in the canal moves with the tide or near slack water. Cape Cod Bay is viewed in the distance on the far side of Cape Cod.

above: Phinney's Harbor and Monument Beach, located on the east side of the Buzzards Bay entrance to the Cape Cod Canal, is okay as an anchorage, provided the weather is settled. The quietest spot is near the marina pictured.

left: The Pocasset River at Bennet's Neck is useful to small shoal draft boats. The bridge clearance a half mile inland from the jetties is seven feet.

below inset: Red Brook Harbor serving Cataumet and Pocasset is a popular anchorage, although it is constantly subject to shoaling. Depending on where and when you enter, you could touch bottom with as little as five feet of draft.

left: Bassetts Island (left) and Scraggy Neck (right) form one of two entrances to Red Brook Harbor. The entrance is most subject to shoaling.

above: Red Brook Harbor's two
boatyards can handle any type
of repair or berthing requirement.
Arrive early to secure overnight
moorings or dockage.

below: Quisset Harbor is safest in the bight at the left. Elsewhere, it is exposed to wind and waves from summer westerly winds. Provisions are scarce, too. Nantucket Sound is in the background.

right: The various anchorages of Woods Hole are all quite popular despite fierce tidal currents in the area. The large open spot, Great Harbor (center), is easiest for strangers to access.

below: From Woods Hole (foreground) the Elizabeth Islands stretch out to the southwest. Anchorages are numerous but tidal currents strong, up to six knots. Gay Head, on Martha's Vineyard is at top left.

above: Hadley Harbor (foreground), on Naushon Island, is a favorite overnight anchorage for boats plying the waters of the southern shores of the Cape and Woods Hole (background).

right: The private Oceanographic Institute is a mainstay at Woods Hole, along with the National Marine Fisheries Service's labs and the U.S. Geological Survey's facilities. Martha's Vineyard is visible in the background.

above: Directly southwest of Woods Hole and enclosed by Nonamesset Island (foreground), Goats Neck (middle left), and Bull Island (middle, right of center), are Hadley Harbor (to the right of Bull Island) and Inner Harbor (to the right of Goats Neck). Naushon Island stretches in the distance.

left: Cuttyhunk Island at the western end of the Elizabeth Islands first gained fame as a whaling port, then fell into decline. It is now an important pleasure boat haven.

below inset: Cuttyhunk Pond has the dubious reputation of being a fine place to run aground. Follow the markers and you should have no problems.

below: Cuttyhunk Island is situated at the southwest end of the Elizabeth Islands. Beyond, barely visible, is the recently replaced Buzzards Bay Tower.

above: No other haven on the Cape's south shore has as many waterfront facilities catering to passing boats as Falmouth Inner Harbor. The anchorage is deep, too.

above: Lewis Neck is on the east side of the curvy Great Pond, accessible only to small boats.

left inset: Green Pond is the next viable harbor eastward of Falmouth. It is small and consequently often crowded. The old bridge with six-foot clearance has been replaced by one with slightly more clearance (under construction when this photo was taken), which still limits cruising boats to the pond's seaward portion.

above: Waquoit Bay is fun mainly for shoal draft boats. There is only one marina on it, but it's relatively roomy for most small boat activities.

right: This photograph shows the inner harbor at Waquoit Bay, including the end of Washburn Island (left) on the west side of the bay.

left: Cotuit Bay is one of the most popular boating havens on the south shore. Most facilities are in Osterville, although the town of Cotuit does have a public pier. Cape Cod Bay is in the background.

below: West Bay offers an alternative route to the facilities at Osterville. There is, however, a bridge that must be opened to take full advantage of the services available.

right inset: Hyannis can partly thank the Kennedy family for its now bustling, busy tourist economy. The Kennedy complex has drawn visitors to the beautiful town and made Hyannis the spot that most people identify as quintessential Cape Cod. The Kennedy Memorial is in Hyannis.

above: The entrance to Lewis Bay from Hyannis Outer Harbor at Dunbar Point (center) is seen with a glimpse of Hyannis Inner Harbor and Cape Cod Bay in the background.

left: A peaceful moment at Hyannis Harbor is rare in this normally bustling tourist town. A crossroads for transportation, both by water and by land, it is attractive to the tourist and resident alike.

below: The entrance to the Bass River is surrounded by sandy beaches and shoals, both of which help make the area true to its namesake, the striped bass.

left: This view of the entrance to Parkers River includes West Yarmouth (left) and at the town of Bass River (right).

left inset: Harwich was a center of fishing on Cape Cod. Located in the Mid-Cape region, it still draws fishermen, and vast summer crowds looking for sun and sea.

above: The entrances to Saquatucket (right) and Wychmere (left) harbors always seem to confuse strangers. Follow your charts carefully and you should avoid a grounding.

right: For a change, Stage Harbor is home to a commercial fishing fleet as well as pleasure vessels. The channel shoals in sometimes, but boats of modest draft have no problems. Stage Harbor leads to Morris Island and the Mitchell River.

left: Oyster Pond River leading to Oyster Pond at Chatham is a nice diversion from Stage Harbor, provided the boat does not draw more than two feet.

below inset: This town has had a thriving fishing industry due to its location—it is almost completely surrounded by water. Located on the "elbow" of Cape Cod, Chatham is subjected to both the bounty and the rage of the sea.

below: The entrance to Stage Harbor from Chatham Roads at Harding Beach and Harding Beach Point are seen with the Atlantic Ocean in the distance.

above: The sun sets at Gay Head, the western extremity of the island of Martha's Vineyard.

right inset: Menemsha Pond and the entrance from Menemsha Bight are on the western side of Martha's Vineyard, just inside Gay Head.

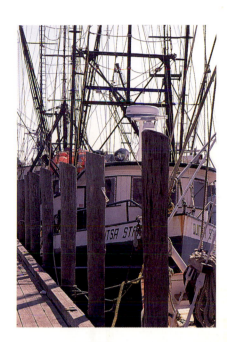

right: Fishing boats still fill the harbor in Menemsha on Martha's Vineyard. The quaint "New England" feel of the town has not been eliminated by summertime visitors; it remains attractive to both artists and fishermen.

below: Vineyard Haven Harbor is busy with ferry traffic from the mainland, pleasure boats, commercial fishing and research boats, and just about anything else that floats.

OAK BLUFFS

On the northeast side of Martha's Vineyard you will find a narrow entrance leading to the well protected "man-made" harbor of Oak Bluffs located in the middle of the town. Here you will find the famous gingerbread houses that surround the tabernacle of this celebrated Methodist meeting ground. At the edge of the harbor, catch a ride on the country's oldest hand-carved flying horses and merry-go-round. A short walk along the edge of the harbor takes you to the sandy beaches and warm waters of Vineyard Sound.

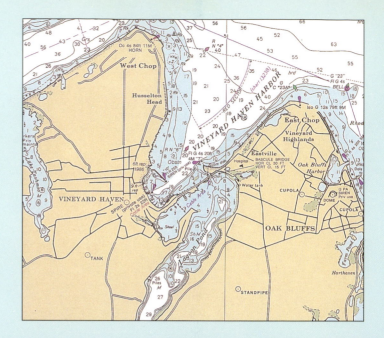

left: The scenic stretches of land around the coast of Martha's Vineyard near Edgartown reveal the impact of the ocean.

below: Edgartown Light marks one side of the entrance to Edgartown with Chappaquiddick Point on the other. Anchoring behind Chappaquiddick Point is a bad idea because of strong tidal currents, a gravelly bottom, and very little swinging room.

right inset: The "gingerbread houses" of Oak Bluffs on Martha's Vineyard are reminders of the Victorian era in which the houses were built. Centered around a religious meeting grounds, the houses were first built to replace tents in which the people stayed during the revivals. The bright colors and ornate decorations were added as neighbors competed for the best Victorian house.

far right inset: Edgartown Lighthouse has guided seamen for over a century. Once a center for the whaling industry, Edgartown is now host to many summer visitors and yachtsmen.

right inset: The streets on the island of Nantucket have changed little since its early days, when wealth from the whaling industry built the seamen's mansions and the cobblestone streets. Today, the old Quaker traditions are maintained on this island about 30 miles from the coast of Cape Cod.

above: Fogs tend to hang around Nantucket early in the sailing season. But once waters warm, the entrance to the harbor is easy, and picturesque as it appears here.

CHAPTER FOUR

MASSACHUSETTS WATERS NORTH OF THE CAPE

NORTHERN CAPE COD TO CAPE ANN, INCLUDING BOSTON HARBOR

Duxbury Bay and Plymouth Harbor

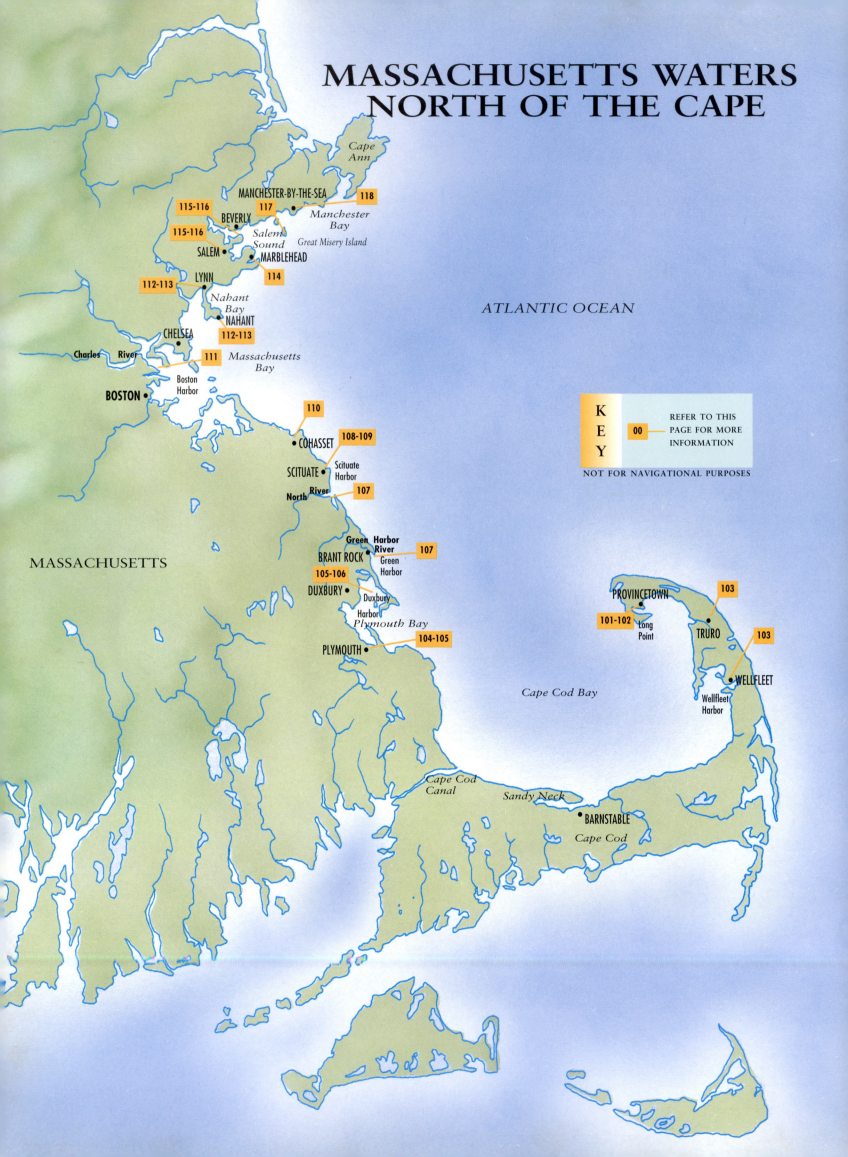

MASSACHUSETTS WATERS NORTH OF THE CAPE

Cape Ann

MANCHESTER-BY-THE-SEA **118**

115-116 BEVERLY **117** *Manchester Bay*

115-116 *Salem Sound* *Great Misery Island*

SALEM MARBLEHEAD

114

LYNN *ATLANTIC OCEAN*

112-113 *Nahant Bay*

CHELSEA NAHANT

112-113

Charles River **111** *Massachusetts Bay*

Boston Harbor

BOSTON

KEY

00 — REFER TO THIS PAGE FOR MORE INFORMATION

NOT FOR NAVIGATIONAL PURPOSES

110

COHASSET **108-109**

SCITUATE *Scituate Harbor*

North River **107**

Green Harbor River **107**
BRANT ROCK Green Harbor

105-106

DUXBURY Duxbury Harbor

Plymouth Bay

PROVINCETOWN **103**

101-102 Long Point

TRURO **103**

104-105

PLYMOUTH WELLFLEET

Wellfleet Harbor

Cape Cod Bay

MASSACHUSETTS

Cape Cod Canal *Sandy Neck*

BARNSTABLE

Cape Cod

above: Provincetown and Long Point (foreground) make up the curling tip of Cape Cod. The bight at Provincetown once harbored hundreds of tall ships waiting for "a chance" to sail around the outer Cape. Today, pleasure and commercial fishing boats share it.

left: The Center Methodist Church in Provincetown, built in 1861, overlooks the long, timbered pier, glistening water, and sandy beaches. The town stands on the site where the Pilgrims first landed in 1620. Today, with its busy wharf and prim Victorian cottages, Provincetown is an artists' colony, fishing town, and summer resort. Artists and writers including Jackson Pollock, Mark Rothko, Eugene O'Neill, and Tennessee Williams have found inspiration here.

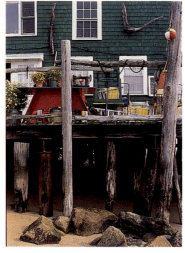

above: Constructed of gray granite, the Pilgrim Monument rises 252 feet from the sandy beach on Provincetown Harbor. The memorial commemorates the Pilgrims' arrival on these shores in 1620 and the Mayflower Contract, the predecessor of the Constitution. On a clear day, the top of the monument offers a spectacular view of the Atlantic and Cape Cod Bay.

above left: Inns, restaurants, and shops are abundant in sandy, wind-swept Provincetown, located at the tip of Cape Cod. Fishermen of Portuguese descent, writers, and artists make up this colorful community.

above right: In the summer, boats connect Boston and "P'town," as Provincetown is know by locals. Fishermen, as in ages past, unload cod, flounder, and mackerel on the wharves. Fishing in Provincetown reached its peak in the late 1800s. A Chicago *Tribune* reporter who visited the town in 1900 wrote: "Fish is bartered at the grocery store, shoe shops and bread stores for all the commodities of life...."

above: Truro Point River is a harbor of limited use. A few miles southeast of Provincetown, it is used by shoal boats in calm weather; though it may be dredged from time to time.

left inset: Authentic fishing boats, sailboats and yachts bob in Wellfleet Harbor. The fishing pier and footbridge over the Duck River add to the charm of this Cape Cod harbor town. Whaling and oystering were once the principal sources of wealth here. Today, fishing continues, but the town's primary source of income is tourism.

above: The shifting sands and strong tidal currents of Wellfleet Harbor make accurate navigation right up to the inner basin at Duck Creek an absolute must.

above: Pleasure boats, a dedicated tuna fishing fleet, and the *Mayflower* find refuge and numerous facilities in the calm waters behind the breakwater at Plymouth Harbor.

right: Plymouth Rock, engraved with the date 1620, commemorates the Pilgrims' arrival on the shores of Massachusetts. The *Mayflower's* passengers, blown off course by storms, landed in Massachusetts rather than their intended destination—Virginia's James River. Only half the Pilgrims survived their first bitter New England winter.

left inset: This colorful replica of the *Mayflower* is moored at State Pier in Plymouth. The seventeenth- century merchant vessel replica is 106 feet long with a 25-foot beam. Of the 102 passengers who traveled on the ship, only four died during the cramped, grueling 66 day voyage.

above: Duxbury (near basin)
and Plymouth (at the top of this
photograph) are the best harbors
of refuge until you reach the
Cape Cod Canal to the south or
Scituate to the north.

above: Duxbury's anchorage basin is a perpetual dredging project. To avoid trouble, ask the harbormaster for a mooring, and avoid anchoring near the edge of the fleet.

above: Winter storms often change the channel into Green Harbor. It's easiest to follow with a shoal draft and rising tide.

left: North River (right) is flanked by the South River, Fourth Cliff (left), and the entrance to the New Inlet. Although it's called New Inlet, it was only new in 1898 when a storm broke through the barrier beach. Today, it includes North and South Rivers, most of which is best left to shoal-draft boats.

above: Scituate Harbor (foreground) is deep, easy to enter, and offers plenty of facilities. It's very handy for anyone cruising around greater Massachusetts Bay.

Trending south from the harbor are the coastal features of First Cliff, Second Cliff, Third Cliff, and, at the entrance to the North and South Rivers, Fourth Cliff.

above: There's plenty of off-season activity at Scituate Harbor with at least one marina operating year-round and an active U.S. Coast Guard station near the entrance. Scituate's back harbor is near the bottom of this photograph with Massachusetts Bay to the north in the background.

right inset: This unoccupied lighthouse is located a short distance south of the harbor entrance and is clearly visible from all approaches to Scituate Harbor. Scituate Lighthouse guards one of the best and largest anchorages from Cape Cod Canal to Boston. In the winter of 1956, in a severe northeast storm, the seven thousand ton *Etrusco* ran aground just in front of Scituate Light. All believed that she was a total loss. With the help of bulldozers, trenches, anchors, and a very high tide, she was dragged to deep water nine months after grounding.

right: The entrance to Cohasset Harbor and Cohasset Cove are shown with Cohasset, Bryant Point, White Head, and Windmill Point. The outer harbor at Cohasset is only useful in calm weather and for fishing for blues and stripers.

left: The inner harbor at Cohasset is safe in all weather, but it tends to be crowded with virtually no swinging room for a boat at anchor. Moorings are usually available.

left inset: Minots Light, an 85-foot lighthouse, was erected in 1860 after an earlier structure slipped into the sea with both lighthouse keepers losing their lives. The first lighthouse was erected by the government after more than forty ships entering and leaving Boston went aground in the early 1800s.

above: This view of Boston Harbor includes downtown Boston, Charlestown, South Boston, Chelsea with Broad Sound, and Massachusetts Bay in the distance.

left inset: Boston Harbor contains a surprising amount of pleasure boat activities and facilities, in addition to fairly heavy ocean going shipping. This scene of Boston includes a look north to Salem Sound, Cape Ann, and the Gulf of Maine.

left: Included in this comprehensive photograph of the North Shore of Boston is Nahant Bay and Marblehead in the foreground, and Salem Sound, Manchester Bay, and Cape Ann (far right) in the distance.

above inset: This view of Nahant and Lynn is what most airborne visitors to Boston see first. Two hundred years ago, new visitors saw the same geography, though from a decidedly different angle.

above: For nearly a hundred years, Marblehead (foreground) and Salem Sound have been a notorious breeding ground of championship racing sailors.

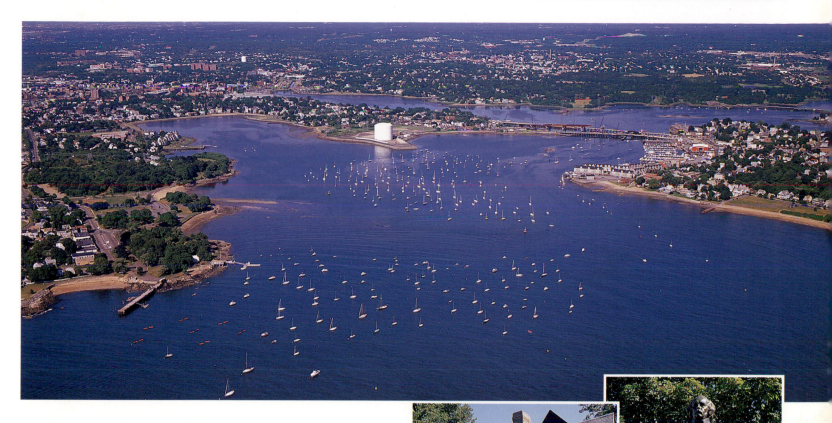

above: Beverly Harbor between Salem Neck and Tuck Point is always busy with pleasure boat and occasional commercial tug traffic.

below: The swing bridges in Beverly Harbor are busy during the summer boating season. Most open on specific schedules so it's best to be patient. The swing bridge on Route 1A is scheduled to be replaced by a stationary bridge, relieving boat and traffic congestion.

above left inset: Nathaniel Hawthorne immortalized the House of Seven Gables in Salem in his book of the same name, written in 1851. The seventeenth century mansion was Hawthorne's cousin's home.

above right inset: A statue of Nathaniel Hawthorne, created by Bela Pratt, stands at the head of Hawthorne Boulevard in Salem. Hawthorne, a Salem native, incorporated many of his memories of Salem life in his writing.

above: Although open to strong winds from the northeast, Salem Harbor is otherwise a good boating area. Naugus Head (left) and Winter Island mark the entrance to the harbor.

right inset: A bronze statue of Roger Conant, the stern Puritan founder of Salem (often mistaken by tourists for a warlock), stands outside a former Salem church that now houses the Witch Museum. Artist Henry Kitson created the statue in 1911. The museum recreates the seventeenth century Salem witch trials.

MISERY ISLAND

Less than three miles northeast of Marblehead Harbor and one mile
east of Manchester Harbor lie Great and Little Misery Islands.
These delightful islands are a convenient and fun pause on your trip
down east. On Great Misery, you can find a small but calm harbor
that offers free moorings. Visitors and locals alike travel there for
swimming, picnicking, and hiking trails, for both day adventures
and overnight trips. Low tide exposes the ruins of an old ship in
the channel between the two islands, but not the wreck of Captain
Moulton, after which the island was named. Many of the locals still
refer to it as "Moulton's Misery." In the 1920s, the islands were the
site of resorts and casinos, where celebrities traveled for a weekend
of fun and gambling. This photograph shows Manchester Harbor
with Misery Island in the background.

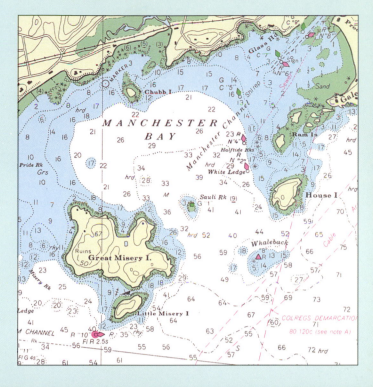

left: Manchester Bay, Manchester Harbor, and Proctor Point are frequently on the "must see" list because of the security and charm of the area.

below right: Shoreside at Manchester-By-The-Sea is just as tightly packed as in the harbor. But the atmosphere in general remains steadfastly easy-going.

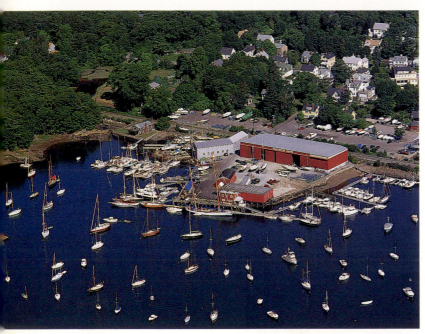

above: Anchoring is impossible in Manchester Harbor, but on weekdays, there's often a vacant mooring or slip. Town dock tie-up is limited to 15 minutes.

right: Behind Kettle Island is Magnolia Harbor and Gray Beach. Offering some breathing room from the crowded overnight harbors, this is a valuable haven in daylight during calm weather.

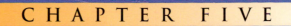

CHAPTER FIVE

NORTHERN MASSACHUSETTS
AND THE
NEW HAMPSHIRE COAST

CAPE ANN TO THE ISLES OF SHOALS

Shown here is the Merrimack River

NORTHERN MASSACHUSETTS AND NEW HAMPSHIRE COASTS

MAINE

ATLANTIC OCEAN

Piscataqua River

KITTERY **130**

PORTSMOUTH
New Castle Island
Little Harbor

129 Isles of Shoals
Appledore Island
Smuttynose Island
Star Island
Cedar Island

Rye Harbor
128

Hampton Beach

NEW HAMPSHIRE

Hampton Harbor **128**

Seabrook Beach

Merrimack River **127**

Joppa Flats

NEWBURYPORT

K E Y
00 REFER TO THIS PAGE FOR MORE INFORMATION

NOT FOR NAVIGATIONAL PURPOSES

Plum Island

Plum Island Sound

Ipswich Bay
126
125-126
LANESVILLE
PIGEON COVE
Sandy Bay

IPSWICH

127 Essex Bay
123
Annisquam Harbor
124-126
ROCKPORT
125
Thatcher Island

ESSEX
Cape Ann
Milk Island

Essex River

MASSACHUSETTS

Annisquam River **123**

GLOUCESTER

Gloucester Harbor **121-123**

Eastern Point

below: Gloucester Harbor dominates Cape Ann (left foreground) with Eastern Point and its trademark breakwater on the right and the town of Rockport (top) in the distant northeast.

right inset: The influx of Portuguese fishermen and their families to the Gloucester area began as early as 1829. The Portuguese community petitioned the Boston archdiocese in 1888 for a parish, and the Our Lady of Good Voyage Church was built a year later.

above: This panorama gives a sweeping view of Gloucester Harbor including Tenpound Island, the city of Gloucester, Rocky Neck, Smiths Cove, and the Inner Harbor.

right inset: The Gloucester Fisherman, created by Leonard Craske, is a landmark of the town harbor. The Fisherman, who stands at the harbor's edge, is said to honor all fishermen lost at sea. Gloucester, founded in 1623, is the country's oldest working fishing port.

THEY THAT GO
DOWN TO THE SEA
IN SHIPS
1623 — 1923

right inset: As this view shows, entering the Annisquam River and Ipswich Bay from the north brings you perilously close to the breakers on the white sands of Wingaersheek Beach.

below: Eliminating the long trip around Cape Ann, the Blynman Canal and Annisquam River are a handy shortcut to Ipswich Bay at the top in the distance.

above: Rockport Harbor is so popular that boats must be moored fore-and-aft to accommodate the crush. Created mainly out of stone, Bearskin Neck and its breakwater are pictured to the lower right. Part of Sandy Bay can be seen at the top right.

right: Thatcher's Island can be seen in the background of this view of Rockport Harbor on Cape Ann.

left: In this view of Thatcher's Island and Milk Island, the twin lights of Thatcher's are easily visible. Only the southernmost one is still in use.

below: This panorama overlooks Granite Pier, Rockport. Just outside Granite Pier is Sandy Bay, offering good holding ground, a picturesque beach, and a pleasant place to stop when the wind is not blowing from the east.

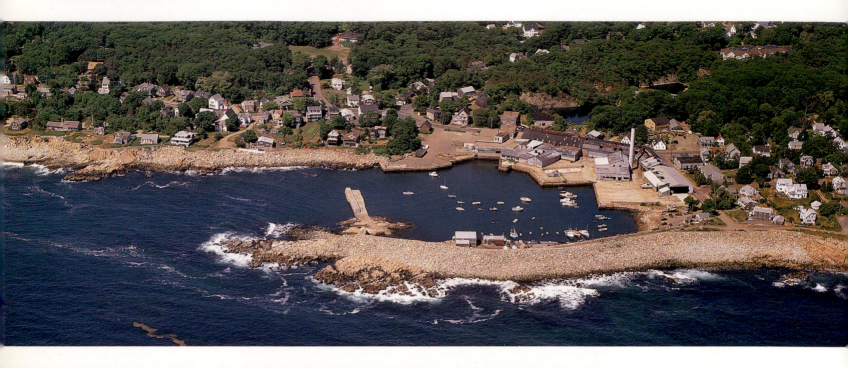

above: Rockport Publishers is visible in the background of this view of Pigeon Cove Harbor, Rockport, the location of a large part of Rockport's fishing fleet.

left: This scene shows Lanes Cove, Lanesville, Plum Cove, and Hodgkins Cove, all located near the entrance to the Annisquam River on Ipswich Bay.

below inset: This old building in Rockport is commonly called "Motif #1" because of the large number of artists who come to paint this characteristic New England coastal fishing shack. It sits on the end of a stone pier in Rockport Harbor, and, to many artists' delight, is framed by the beautiful blue expanse of the Atlantic Ocean.

right: The Essex River channel shifts occasionally, but it's usually well marked and always worth the effort. There's good swimming from the white sands of Coffin Beach (top) and Castle Neck, plus good fishing in Essex Bay (right).

left: The jetties at the Merrimack River entrance to Newburyport Harbor have improved navigation, but you still have to be wary of the strong tidal currents.

below left: Those tidal currents remain strong right up to the docks in downtown Newburyport. But it's worth the trip as the town has made a big effort to welcome passing sailors.

below inset: The Maritime Museum in historic Newburyport provides a unique permanent collection of ship models, maritime paintings, and interesting artifacts pertaining to maritime life. This museum, offering a variety of activities, features changing exhibits, book signings, and a number of other educational programs.

above: Hampton Harbor and its beaches, north and south, draw thousands every summer. In a shoal draft boat, the Hampton River in the background is one place to escape the crowds.

right: Recently redredged, Rye Harbor is popular with sport fishermen and rapidly spreading its reputation for easy access and tight space.

ISLES OF SHOALS

Just eight miles at sea east of the coastal town of Portsmouth, New Hampshire, divided by the state line between New Hampshire and Maine, you will find the seven Isles of Shoals, including Appledore, Smuttynose, Star, and more that offer hiking, bird rookeries, famous gardens, swimming, interesting history in the form of headstones, plaques, and monuments, an observation tower from World War II, historic buildings, several gruesome stories, as well as the remote and traditional "down east" anchorage of Gosport Harbor. All of this, and available almost directly on your route down east or by ferry from Portsmouth.

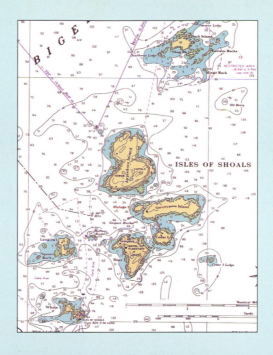

left: Wentworth-by-the-Sea Marina has made Little Harbor into a large and popular haven for transient and permanent mariners. Portsmouth is visible at right, in the background.

below inset: The Portsmouth Harbor area is worth a visit of several days, including a trip with the tide up the Piscataqua River to Great Bay in the distant background.

left inset: The USS *Albacore* was built in 1953 in the nearby Portsmouth Naval Shipyard. Today, it is open to the public, offering an inside look at how its crew of 55 men lived and worked aboard the 205 Submarine.

right: Fisherman's Pier in Portsmouth, New Hampshire is across from the historic Strawbery Banke and public gardens. The tiny, picturesque wharf is used predominantly by the local fishermen.

CHAPTER SIX

THE SOUTHERN MAINE COAST

YORK HARBOR TO MONHEGAN, INCLUDING CASCO BAY

Shown here is Cape Neddick

THE SOUTHERN MAINE COAST

MAINE

BELFAST

Moose Point

Northport

Lincolnville

CAMDEN
ROCKPORT

Damariscotta
Lake

LEWISTON

WALDOBORO

ROCKLAND
THOMASTON

Owls Head

VINAL

Newcastle

151

Broad Cove

Cushing
Saint George

WISCASSET

145-150

Edgecomb

FRIENDSHIP

Spruce Head

Woolwich

Bristol

Tenants Harbor

144-145

Walpole Round Pond

142

BRUNSWICK **143**

BATH
Sheepscot
River

Boothbay

Pemaquid

151

PORT CLYDE

New Harbor

152-153

Desert of Maine

YARMOUTH

Sebascodegan
Island

Phippsburg

Southport
Island

146-149

Matinicus Island

New Meadows River

Georgetown

Muscongus Bay

Ragged Island

Harpswell

Orrs Island

Parker Head

Chebeague
Island

143

Popham Beach

Monhegan Island

FALMOUTH

Jewell
Island

Bailey Island

144-145

154

WESTBROOK

141

142

Small Point Beach

PORTLAND

139-140

Casco Bay

Portland Head Light

Two Lights

139-140

CAPE ELIZABETH

SACO

PROUTS NECK

BIDDEFORD

OLD ORCHARD BEACH

139

SPRINGVALE

138

Saco Bay

SANFORD

138

KENNEBUNK

BIDDEFORD POOL

KENNEBUNKPORT

BERWICK

136-137

SOMERSWORTH

Wells
Beach

135

Perkins Cove

135

CAPE NEDDICK

ELIOT

134

YORK

KITTERY **133**

Fort K

Sec
Isla

Penobscot Bay

North
Isla

Gr
Isl

above: This view of the York Harbor entrance shows the York River, Stage Neck, and Bragdon Island in the background. A ferocious tidal current makes it a challenge to get to the perfect protection and excellent boating facilities in York Harbor, just beyond Stage Neck.

right inset: Six miles east of York Harbor and annually swept by storm waves, Boon Island welcomes boaters to Maine with its forbidding look of nobility. The island is known for an incident of cannabalism to serve the need for survival that occurred there.

above: The Nubble Lighthouse is seen in this view of Cape Neddick Nubble. The coves and beaches near Cape Neddick and Nubble Lighthouse are ideal for boats only if the seas are calm and the wind offshore.

right: Creating some confusion for many, Cape Neddick Light (the official name) is often called Nubble Light. It sits on a rocky, prominent islet called Cape Neddick Nubble, a few hundred yards seaward of Cape Neddick proper. It is among the most photographed, and misnamed, lighthouses on the Maine coast.

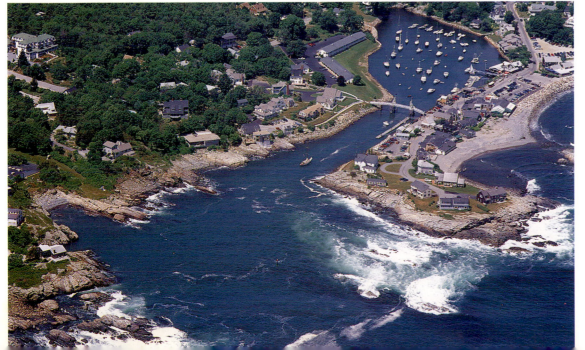

above: This scene shows the entrance to Wells Harbor, Wells Beach, and the Webhannet River. With a shoal draft boat and a rising tide, the trip into Wells Harbor brings boaters to a true tourist's mecca.

left: Perkins Cove at Ogunquit is as crowded as it looks, but the harbormaster is always willing to try to fit one more in.

above: This scene includes the entrance to Kennebunkport, Kennebunk Harbor, and Kennebunk River with Goochs Beach. Even without a sitting president in residence, the beaches, rivers, and harbors of Kennebunkport are entertaining and busy every summer, all summer.

left: For architecture buffs, a stop in Kennebunkport is worthwhile. Rent a car to see buildings like the Wedding Cake House on State Route 9A/35, a few miles west of town. Built in 1826 by George W. Bourne, the local ship-builder spent 30 years or so adding various whimsical touches to the Gothic Revival building. Excellent examples of Queen Anne, Italianate, Greek Revival and other styles are well docu-mented at the Kennebunkport Historical Society. Most are with-in walking distance of the harbor.

above: In this view of Cape Porpoise Harbor and Trott Island, the Great Island Lighthouse and Horn are visible on the east side. Cape Porpoise makes up for its lack of recreational boating facilities with excellent protection from storm, and a fleet devoted solely to lobstering.

above: Cape Porpoise appears in the background of this view of Biddeford Pool and Wood Island Harbor. If tightly packed Biddeford Pool has no spare moorings, the anchorage between the Pool and Wood Island (foreground) is comfortable in settled weather.

left: This scene shows Prout's Neck on Saco Bay with the entrance to the Scarborough River. Elegant and exclusive by nature and by design, Prout's Neck offers a good anchorage and even better gunkholing in the Scarborough River beyond.

left: Although Richmond Island off Cape Elizabeth is reportedly haunted, there's nothing scary about the anchorages in nearby Seal Cove and Richmond Harbor.

above: This view of Falmouth Foreside, including Princes Point and Clapboard Island, looks out to the channel and the Atlantic. Between Falmouth Foreside and Clapboard Island nests one of the largest fleets of recreational boats in Maine, a top anchorage and attraction.

right: South Portland, Portland, Cushing Island, Portland Harbor, and Portland Inner Harbor are captured in this photograph. Portland Harbor waters are heavy with commercial and recreational traffic all summer, day and night, seven days a week.

left: This sweeping panorama includes Casco Bay and Hussey Sound with Falmouth Foreside, Clapboard Island, and Great Diamond Island in the distance. Running between Peaks Island (left) and Long Island (right), Hussey Sound is the best entrance to Casco Bay if you want to avoid Portland Harbor traffic, and possibly see the start or finish of the Monhegan Race.

left: Merepoint Neck appears on the left in this view of Birch Island on Merepoint Bay. Although shallow, Merepoint Bay remains a popular area because it generally lacks the strong currents and thick fogs found elsewhere in Casco Bay.

above inset: This scene shows Falmouth Foreside and the Portland Yacht Club. The yacht club, a five-star restaurant and excellent boating facilities are among the reasons so many boats congregate at Falmouth Foreside.

JEWELL ISLAND

Entering Casco Bay from the Gulf of Maine, Jewell is one of the first islands encountered. The harbor at this state park is well protected from the south, east, and west. Because of the convenient location and the hiking trails, swimming, and sightseeing, it is often crowded on weekends in the summer months. On Jewell Island you will find many grown over roads that have become pleasant hiking trails leading to tall lookout towers on the south end. Near the towers are several linked tunnels, which supported guns that protected the entrance to Portland Harbor during World War II. After viewing the great panorama of Casco Bay's 365 Calendar Islands from the lookout towers, return to the north end on the eastern, ocean side of the island and swim in the Punch Bowl, with its sandy beach. It fills with Maine's cold water at high tide, and then warms up for your swimming pleasure as the tide recedes.

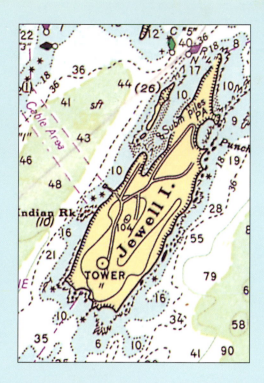

above: Cundy's Harbor on Sebascodegan Island (right), is a good place to begin exploring the New Meadows River (left) or find an inexpensive lobster dinner.

right: In this scene, South Freeport is visible along with the entrance to the Harraseeket River through Stockbridge Point and Moore Point on the north side of Casco Bay. The tiny island called "Pound of Tea" marks the entrance to the Harraseeket River and the boating/shopping mecca of South Freeport and Freeport.

right: From The Basin on the east side of Casco Bay we look to the west over the New Meadows River and Sebascodegan Island. The entrance to The Basin feels like a creek, but the anchorage itself on weekdays is your own private Mill Pond at the east end of Casco Bay.

left: Bailey Island (foreground) and Orrs Island are strung together with Sebascodegan Island (far distance) by road.

right inset: Ancient wrecks can be found all along the coast of Maine. But the greatest concentration is in the Sheepscot Bay area: one on the east side at Robinhood Cove, two at Wiscasset Harbor (pictured); and two on the north side of Goose Rock Passage. All generate fascinating stories of a time—in some cases, not so long ago—when Maine was home to a lot of rough characters.

above: Robinhood Marina, Newdick Point (right foreground), and the western end of Goose Rock Passage lead to the Sheepscot River. Tide rips and whirlpools are common in Goose Rock Passage until you get to the calmer waters of Riggs Cove, with its marina and five-star restaurant.

right: This view shows Cozy Harbor on Southport Island off the Sheepscot River. Cozy Harbor is a quiet little hole-in-the-wall anchorage with few facilities and lots of personality.

left: With a marina, a take-out eatery and an active fishing fleet, Five Islands Harbor is good shelter directly opposite Hendrick Head Light in the Sheepscot River.

right: The Cuckholds and Cape Newagen Harbor mark the eastern extremity of Sheepscot Bay and its abundance of rivers, coves, and harbors. The Cuckholds on the southern end of Cape Newagen split Sheepscot Bay into the Sheepscot River (left) and Booth Bay (right).

above: Cape Harbor at Cape Newagen on Southport Island, appears opposite the Cuckolds with Squirrel Island and Boothbay and Boothbay Harbor in the background. Although beset by a gentle roll at high tide, Cape Harbor offers a handy escape from the hubbub of nearby Boothbay Harbor.

right: If you cannot find it in Boothbay Harbor, it probably doesn't exist. Maine's busiest yachting center has a little bit of everything for every kind of sailor.

above: The cove at the Boothbay
Harbor Yacht Club, off to one
side of the busy harbor, offers
a relatively quiet refuge and
congenial company.

above: The pedestrians-only
footbridge at the head of
Boothbay Harbor's main cove
conveniently links the east and
west sides of town.

right: This panorama of
Boothbay looks north over the
entrance. The greater Boothbay
Harbor area never really fills up
with boats, docked, anchored or
moored. There's always room
at this inn.

right: This view of East Boothbay boatyard on the Damariscotta River looks across to Linekin Bay, Boothbay Harbor, and the Sheepscot River. The boatbuilding center of East Boothbay keeps up a 200-year-old tradition as well as providing ordinary marina services and quiet shelter.

below: Just opposite The Gut on the Damariscotta River, Farnham Cove offers the best protection of any anchorage in East Boothbay.

left inset: Townsend Gut is the quick and easy link between Sheepscot Bay and Boothbay Harbor. The bridge opens on demand.

left: Top-drawer yachts of all description make it a point to stop at the superb facilities of Christmas Cove on Rutherford Island, Damariscotta River.

below: New Harbor, on the east side of Pemaquid Neck, splits into two equally well-protected coves.

above: South Bristol, with Rutherford on the right and Johns Bay in the background, is clustered around the harbor formed by The Gut, a tide-scoured, two-part channel on which the bridge opens on demand.

above: Made famous by nineteenth century sailing great Captain Joshua Slocum, Round Pond still offers perfect protection from all storms plus amenities.

left inset: Mostly a working lobsterman's haven, Friendship Harbor looks out at Muscongus Bay with its coves and harbors. Hatchet Cove is to the right.

left inset: Friendship sloops were the workboats of mid-coast Maine for much of the nineteenth century. Lobstering, fishing and hauling light cargo were among the jobs these handy boats performed. They are still around today, mostly as pleasure boats. A regatta for Friendships has been held annually at Friendship, Boothbay or Rockland harbors.

above: The best anchorage in Port Clyde is in its eastern coves, which afford easy access to the accomodating town. The approaches are studded with thousands of lobsterpots—jewels to the eye, hazards to the propeller.

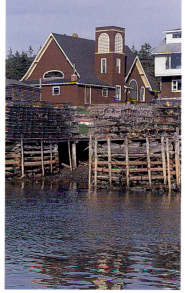

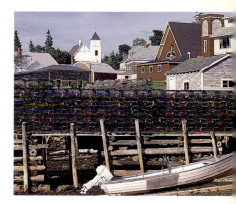

above three images: Port Clyde enjoys an easy harmony between working fishermen and recreational boating enthusiasts. The Port Clyde General Store wharf, where yachtsmen are welcome to tie up, is also a temporary storage area for thousands of lobster traps. The town is also home to the service boat for Monhegan Island. Year-round, it carries passengers, mail, and general cargo eight miles offshore to the 80 or so permanent residents on the island. For side trips into Muscongus Bay, Port Clyde is an indispensable base.

left inset: More than 400 species of wildflowers grow on Monhegan Island. Monhegan Island mixes lobstermen and artists with a strong dose of tourists, coming out no worse for the wear.

below: Monhegan Island is nine miles off Maine's mid-coast. The harbor between Monhegan and Manana Islands is best approached in calm or northerly weather. Anchoring is recommended, as moorings are scarce.

right inset: Manana Island, to the west of Monhegan Island, was for years home to a hermit who subsisted on goat farming and fishing.

CHAPTER SEVEN

THE EASTERN MAINE COAST

OWL'S HEAD TO EASTPORT,
INCLUDING PENOBSCOT BAY AND
MOUNT DESERT ISLAND

Northeast Harbor

THE EASTERN MAINE COAST

MAINE

BANGOR

Fort Knox
BUCKSPORT

ELLSWORTH

Surry

Fort Pownall
Moose Point
BELFAST
Sears Island
166
Northport
Islesboro Island
167
Castine
BLUE HILL

Lincolnville
170-171
Eggemoggin
170-171
Little Deer Island
Sedgwick
Brooklin
175

CAMDEN
160-163
Butter Island
Eagle Island
Stonington
168-169
Penobscot Bay
North Haven Island
Deer Isle
Rockport

ROCKLAND
159
Owls Head
VINALHAVEN
Isle Au Haut Bay
164-165
Green Island
Spruce Head
157-158
Isle Au Haut
168-169

Matinicus Island
Seal Island
Wooden Ball Island
Ragged Island
Criehaven

172-173
Trenton
Lamoine
Hancock Point

BAR HARBOR
179
Mt. Desert
Acadia
178
Sorrento
National Park
CADILLAC MTN
Northeast Harbor
Southwest Harbor
175
Tremont
Somes Sound
176
178
Bass Harbor
177
Swans Island
174
Frenchboro
Long Island
Jericho Bay

181
Cherryfield
Narraguagus River
Harrington
Addison
MILBRIDGE
Dyer Island
Pleasant Bay

WINTER HARBOR
Prospect Harbor
Birch Harbor
Corea
Schoodic Point
180
PETIT MANAN POINT
Frenchman Bay
179

MACHIAS
Machiasport
Bucks Harbor
Roque Bluffs
Roque Island
Machias Bay
183-184
182
183
Jonesport
181
Chandler Bay
Great Wass Island
Cutler

Pembroke
Perry
186-18[?]
EASTPORT
Dennisville
Cobscook Bay
LUBEC
Moosehorn National Wildlife Refuge
186
185

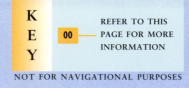

above: Although it looks like a hodgepodge of islands, Muscle Ridge Channel is a safe, easy passageway to Rockland (top left) and Penobscot Bay. Tenants Harbor is in the foreground.

right: Two Bush Lighthouse warns ocean-going ships of the labyrinth of islands and channels that make up Muscle Ridge Channel to the west. Most ships stay in Two Bush Channel when headed for Searsport or Winterport in upper Penobscot Bay.

above: Knox County Airport, on Owl's Head, is visible behind Muscle Ridge Channel.

right: The lofty grounds of Owl's Head Light near Rockland are open to the public, but the parking and the hours are extremely limited. Guest moorings are available in nearby Owl's Head Harbor and the walk is easy.

above: The breakwater at Rockland Harbor protects and separates the harbor from the waters and islands of Penobscot Bay. With an easy entrance, Rockland Harbor has become home to hundreds of yachtsmen and a handful of "dude" schooners in recent years.

right: The 4200-foot breakwater and Rockland Breakwater Light were built after fishermen, merchant windjammers, and wharf owners got tired of easterly storms damaging the harbor's commercial prospects. Today, the sheltered harbor provides protection and various boating services.

left inset: Rockport's ancient lime kilns are a reminder of a crucial nineteenth century industry the town has all but forgotten. The kilns needed 30 cords of wood for burning off solidifying chemicals in limestone to produce a barrel of powdered lime.

below: This scene shows Rockport, home to several schools for artists and artisans, not to mention being a good harbor.

above: Camden Harbor is barely visible a few miles up the coast from Rockport Harbor, and the popular hiking trails in the Camden Hills overlook both harbors.

right inset: The old lighthouse on Indian Island at Rockport has turned over its job to a modern light tower on Lowell Rock immediately to the south of the old location. Entering the harbor from the east, the new light is less likely to lead a vessel onto the rocks.

left: The snug harbor, slightly rolling outer anchorage, and scores of amenities all allow Camden to play host to hundreds of yachts at a time, as this scene reveals.

below left and lower: A long history of being jammed with vessels of all sorts makes Camden a town that deals easily with today's extra traffic. During the nineteenth century, scores of ships up to 300 feet in length were launched without problems into the small harbor.

below right: The Megunticook Falls in the middle of town provided mill power. Today the nearby Camden-Rockport Historical Society offers a free map for a downtown walking tour of sites of interest. Brew pubs, boutiques, and specialty food stores now huddle near the falls, and the town's numerous restaurants have made a new twentieth century industry.

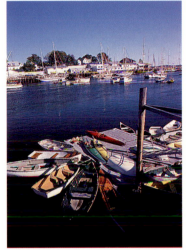

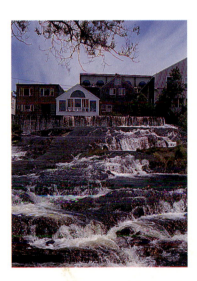

above: Looking west, the convenient cross-bay channel of Fox Islands Thorofare divides North Haven on the right from Vinalhaven on the left.

right: Looking southeast to northwest, this view includes Carver's Harbor on Vinalhaven Island, but there are dozens of other well-protected anchorages around the island.

above: The town of Vinalhaven is at Carver's Harbor on Vinalhaven Island. Regular ferry service to the mainland arrives via the Reach, and lobstering is the order of every day.

left: Browns Head Light at the western entrance to Fox Islands Thorofare sees its share of windjammers out of nearby Camden, Rockport, and Rockland. Automated in 1987, the fog signal was changed from a bell to a horn. The bell was given to the town of Vinalhaven for display.

165

below: This view captures Belfast, Belfast Bay and the Passagassawaukeaq River. Belfast's harbor, once fallen on hard times, has been revived in recent years and now regularly attracts yachtsmen to upper Penobscot Bay.

right: As with many colonial towns in New England, the First Congregational Church in Belfast was among the first buildings constructed. Completed in 1765, its tower is visible from all over northern Penobscot Bay and is a critical landmark on many old charts.

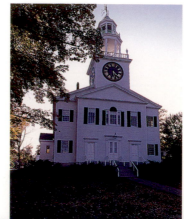

above: With the Maine Maritime Academy in residence, Castine marks the point where Penobscot Bay turns into the long channel of the Penobscot River to Bangor. Here we look eastward across the harbor to Bagaduce River.

right: Frequent fogs make the numerous islands of Deer Isle Thorofare and Merchant Row, as seen in this view, look quite similar, forcing many pleasure boats to pursue other routes eastward.

below: Overlooking Stonington, the hills of Mt. Desert can be seen in the east. Once a quarry town, Stonington now boasts one of the biggest boat repair facilities in the Penobscot Bay region—Billings Marine (foreground).

above: The Fox Islands Thorofare lies to the west, and beyond that, West Penobscot Bay, the Muscle Ridge islands (top left) and the Camden Hills (top right). Stonington is a good base from which to explore the Isle Au Haut to the south and Jericho Bay to the east.

left inset: Many pleasure boats choose this route up Eggemoggin Reach, with Naskeag Point on the right, when other east-west routes to the south are too foggy.

below: Blue Hill Bay looms in the background of this view of Center Harbor, Brooklin, and Eggemoggin Reach. A mecca for wooden boat enthusiasts, Center Harbor is home to the magazine and school that try to keep the old ways of boatbuilding alive.

right: Shown with Cape Rosier in the distance, the northwestern end of Eggemoggin Reach has a fixed bridge, little current and generally good cross breezes.

left: The Benjamin River, located off Eggemoggin Reach, plays host to many vintage wooden yachts, as well as offering excellent anchorage under all conditions.

below: Big passenger schooners often stop at Buck Harbor in South Brooksville off the Eggemoggin Reach. Many head for the local variety store which once sold frozen January snowballs in July, just for fun.

above: Blue Hill Harbor and Blue Hill appear in the background and Parker Point is seen on the left. Chamber concerts, coffee emporiums, and art studios make Blue Hill Harbor a decidedly different haven in Maine.

right inset: Sunrise at Mount Desert Island is more than just a captivating experience. If you climb to the island's highest peak, Cadillac Mountain, you will be the first person in the continental United States to see the sunrise. The walk up is easy, but be prepared for cold, even in mid-July.

above: The Holt House is just one of the historically significant sites in Blue Hill. The town's public library has a hand-and-plate vest worn by Ferdinand Magellan,

Kneisel Hall has been offering chamber music for decades, and the Blue Hill Fair is an annual reminder of the nineteenth century in which the town grew up.

above: A view of the Rockefeller Mansion and boathouse on Seal Harbor. Seal Harbor offers the closest access to the paths that weave among the 35,000 acres of Acadia National Park, the nation's second most popular preserve.

below: Looking east, this scene shows Casco Passage and the south side of Blue Hill Bay. Although relatively benign in clear weather, Casco Passage's cross currents and dual channels can be confusing in fog.

above: Looking northeast, Bartlett Island and Mount Desert Island lie on either side of Bartlett Narrows. On a clear day, Pretty Marsh Harbor (the western reaches of which can be glimpsed at right) is an anchorage from which you can see the peaks of the Camden Hills, Mount Desert Island, and Isle Au Haut.

above: Burnt Coat Harbor on Swans Island is easy to enter and find anchorage. Large windjammers often come and go here, under sail alone.

below: Salmon farming is a growth industry in Maine, as these salmon pens near Swans Island attest. Give them a wide berth, particularly in fog.

above inset: Although it looks lonely, Mount Desert Rock is active during the summer whale watching season. The College of the Atlantic in Bar Harbor situates researchers here and whale watching boats from the mainland regularly ply these waters 15 miles offshore. The 58-foot granite light tower is automated.

above: This view of Bass Harbor includes Southwest Harbor in the distance to the northeast. Although named for a fish that rarely visits, Bass Harbor is still a good anchorage with plenty of shoreside facilities and access to Acadia National Park.

left: Great and Little Cranberry Islands lie to the southeast of Southwest Harbor. Home to a major US Coast Guard station, Hinckley Yachts, and a pleasant little fishing town, Southwest Harbor features a variety of boating activities.

above: The town of Northeast Harbor runs a good—if tight—anchorage, complete with town dockage, showers, moorings, and numerous restaurants.

left: In the shadow of Cadillac Mountain, Northeast Harbor is the hub of yachting activity down east, including visiting windjammers.

SOMES SOUND

Often described as the largest fjord on the east coast of the United States, Somes Sound has mountains lining each side of its deep water channel. Sailing the seven miles up Somes Sound is a peak experience. A place to pause is Valley Cove, the first niche on the west side. Here you can anchor or pick up one of the park service's free moorings. Row ashore to one of the hiking trails that will take you to the summit of Saint Sauveur Mountain for an unforgettable view. Take a trail to Acadia Mountain, or perhaps visit the wildflower gardens of Fernald Point or take a freshwater dip in Echo Lake. At the northern end of Somes Sound there is a well-protected harbor, with excellent repair facilities, plus it's only a short hike to the paved road and Fernald's general store.

left: Champlain Mountain sits behind Bar Harbor in this view. Bar Harbor's streets are even busier than its harbor. As a tourist magnet for nearby Acadia National Park, it offers every amenity imaginable. The ferry *Bluenose* departs Bar Harbor to Yarmouth, Nova Scotia each day.

below inset: Hotels, motels and bed-and-breakfast accommodations in Bar Harbor fill up early in the season. If meeting someone else, call well ahead of arrival.

left: Sand Beach at Newport Cove near Bar Harbor may look inviting, but the water rarely gets warmer than 55 degrees.

above: The coves of Winter Harbor are very rolly in most any southerly wind unless you anchor in the Inner Harbor. Check your depths carefully.

left: Schoodic Peninsula offers relief for anyone tired of the crowds at Acadia National Park on Mount Desert. It too is a part of the park, but rarely visited and quiet even in mid-summer.

below inset: Difficult to reach, Petit Manan Light marks one of the most active tern colonies on the Maine coast. Several varieties of the bird were restored to the island's Petit Manan Wildlife Refuge in the 1980s. Landing is advised only after breeding season ends in late July. Beware of strong currents and rough seas even in summer weather.

above: Frenchman Bay can be seen on the other side of the Schoodic Peninsula in this view of Prospect Harbor.

right: The larger water of Gouldsboro Bay lies behind Corea Harbor, where Marsden Hartley summered and painted in his later years.

left: A bridge crosses Moosabec Reach connecting Jonesport to Beals Island which in turn is connected by road to Great Wass Island.

JAMES W. SEWALL CO.

below inset: This scene shows the split in Narraguagus Bay, and the left branch becomes the entrance to the Narraguagus River.

below: A look westward from Jonesport reveals the convoluted islands, inlets, and harbors of Maine's coast.

right inset: Moose Peak Light marks two channels leading into a maze of islands, coves, and lakes with unique natural beauty. Pirates, ghosts, and buried treasure are stories connected with Head Harbor and Steele Harbor Islands to the northeast. The Nature Conservancy protects the subarctic plants and geologic formations called "thunder holes" on nearby lower Great Wass Island.

above: Englishman Bay is visible behind Great Spruce Island and Roque Island, and beyond that the mainland blueberry barrens, crimson in autumn.

right inset: A high altitude photograph of Little Machias Bay.

JAMES W. SEWALL CO.

far left: Machiasport and the entrance to the Machias River are captured in this scene.

left: Avery Rock Light and Sprague Neck lie in the sandy and island-dotted Machias Bay.

below: Cutler Peninsula, between Machias Bay and Little Machias Bay, can be clearly identified by its large array of radio towers.

JAMES W. SEWALL CO.

JAMES W. SEWALL CO.

below: This scene shows Little River and Little River Island with Cutler and Little Machias Bay in the distance to the west.

left: Almost tropical in the coloring on their beaks, puffins are anything but a warmth-loving bird. Found only on remote off-shore islands—Eastern Egg Rock in Muscongus Bay, Matinicus Rock in lower Penobscot Bay and Machias Seal Island off Machias Bay—puffins spend a brief summer in Maine and then winter at sea near the ice line in the North Atlantic. Shy and skittish, they are best seen with binoculars from a boat.

JAMES W. SEWALL CO.

above: West Quoddy Head is connected to the mainland only by a small strip of land. West Quoddy Head Light sits alone on the eastern end of the land.

above inset: A high altitude view of West Quoddy Head.

left: Looking over West Quoddy Head toward Lubec Neck and Johnson Bay.

above: Lubec Narrows splits Lubec Neck from Campobello Island near the city of Lubec. Eastport (right) can be seen in the near background.

right: The waters of Friar Roads pass Eastport (top center) and Seward Neck (left) and then travel down to Lubec.

far right: Eastport on Moose Island is in the center of this view with the Western Passage and Deer Island to the north.

above: Eastport sits on the southeastern end of Moose Island.

left inset: The pens at Eastport give evidence of the thriving salmon culture industry. Cobscook Bay's 25-foot tides keep the pens clean and well oxygenated.

above: A view of Eastport from the south shows Friar Roads to the east, the western passage to the northwest, and Deer Island, New Brunswick, to the north.

right: The waters of Cobscook Bay are split by Hersey Neck to the northwest and Sewards Neck to the southeast.

JAMES W. SEWALL CO.

WHILE GATHERING THE PARTICULARS for this book, indispensable help and support came from many directions. My wife, Doris, gave her usual warm support, encouragement, and space to help me pull it all together.

This book could not have been made without the talented, supportive staff at Rockport Publishers. They worked on the Coastal Guide while they assembled at least thirty other visual books. Thanks to Shawna Mullen and her colleagues for editorial support; to Lynne Havighurst for design help; and to Barbara States and Pat O'Maley for supervising the full-color photographic duplication and book production.

There were many people who gave long hours and much effort to make this book a reality. A special recognition to Alexandra Bahl who coordinated and nurtured all of the many pieces, including the author and production staff through the creation of this book. Thanks to Ken Textor, an author, editor, and sea captain from the state of Maine, who added his coastal knowledge, writing, and editing skills to this mix; and to Kathy Kelley, for her unflagging efforts, creativity, and patience in the design of this book.

My friend, official pilot, and advisor, Ron Harnish, helped to make the Coastal Guide to New England come to life with his piloting skill and his in-depth knowledge of the New England coast. In addition to the breathtaking photography of Laurence Lowry, we have included photography from Arthur Furst, Elizabeth Smith, Carolyn Bearce, Lisa Patey, and Bonnie Burke. The maps were created by Janos Marffy and Brenda Waslick. Thanks to Foster Shibles, who worked with the James W. Sewall Company in Bangor, Maine, to select high altitude photography of sections of northern Maine.

Our labor of love was commissioned by International Marine, who made the decision to publish the Coastal Guide to New England. Finally, great thanks to Laurence Orbach and his colleagues at our mother company, Quarto, who empower all of us to spend our time creating beautiful books.